10650034

❝Strange acrobatics of a human ball curled up in a strange dance, provocative and artistic, which does not stand comparison to any other dance in the world, ever.❞

Vicente Rossi, 1926

For their help, Maizal would like to thank Nené Weil, Nicolás Rubió, Esther Barugel, Eduardo Ungar, Georgie Berczely, David J. J. Bellis and Omar Sosa and Cristina Fontana.

Other Books Published by MAIZAL

Spanish/Español
El Mate
El Gaucho
Argentina Natural
La Cocina Argentina
Vinos Argentinos
Indígenas Argentinos
Textiles Argentinos
Carne Argentina
El Tango
El Filete Porteño
Tiempo de Té

English/Inglés
The Mate
The Gaucho
Argentine Nature
Argentine Cookery
Argentine Wines
Argentine Indians
Argentine Textiles
Argentine Beef

Bilingual/Bilingüe
Teatro Colón
Pintura Argentina/
Argentine Painting
Buenos Aires Viaje/
Buenos Aires Journey

Argentrip
Argentina's on-line travel guide
www.argentrip.com

Book and Cover Design: Christian le Comte and Sophie le Comte
© Mónica G. Hoss de le Comte, 2000

Hecho el depósito que previene la ley 11.723
I.S.B.N. 987-97899-2-X
Published by Maizal
Muñíz 438, B1640FDB, Martínez
Buenos Aires, Argentina.
E-mail: info@maizal.com
www.maizal.com
Printed in June 2005 by Morgan Internacional

Mónica Gloria Hoss de le Comte

The Tango

MAIZAL
EDICIONES

The Word Tango

Tango is a word of African origin. In some African dialects the word means closed meeting–place.

At the end of the eighteenth century the slaves called tango the place where they met to make music and dance.

"*Mi Buenos Aires Querido*"
Carlos Gardel

Candombe

In 1770 the Viceroy Juan José Vertiz issued a decree to limit the excesses of these social gatherings that had developed from quiet meetings into noisy parties.

It has also been said that the word *tan–go* imitates the beat of percussion instruments, used to mark the rhythm of a dance called *candombe*.

The candombe was a dance of complicated and improvised choreography and with a strongly marked rhythm. It was danced separately and the dancers made all sorts of contortions. These movements were then imitated by the *compadritos* (see page 22) to poke fun at the slaves and they used them later on when they danced the tango.

"*El día que me quieras*"
Carlos Gardel

The History of Tango

> *"At the beginning it was an orgiastic mischief,*
> *today it is a way of walking."*
> Jorge Luis Borges, 1930

"La Taba"
A. Villoldo · A. Bellomo
Sheet Music Cover

"Sacudime la per-siana"
V. Loduca

"Mi noche triste"
P. Contursi · S Castriota

The history of tango starts around the year 1870, when, in the suburbs of Buenos Aires, dances and songs of different origins came together.

The Cuban seamen who sailed the commercial route between the Caribbean Sea and the Río de la Plata brought the *habanera*, a slow dance in $\frac{2}{4}$ time.

The *payadas*, improvisations that the *gauchos* sung with the guitar, had become *milongas* when they got to the suburbs of the city. The milonga became a very popular dance and it is regarded nowadays as the nearest ancestor of the tango.

But the tango doesn't only have the blood of habaneras, payadas and milongas.

In the second half of the nineteenth century, Spanish theatre companies came to Buenos Aires and they included habaneras and Andalusian tangos in their plays. The Andalusian tango was a variation of the habanera but more cheerful and light–hearted.

To all this, one has to add the contribution of the slaves and their *candombes*, their pulsing rhythm and improvised steps and that of the Italian immigrants who loved to sing and were able to play instruments.

The tango then was born in the suburbs of Buenos Aires. It has something of the candombe, much of the habanera, traces of milongas and Andalusian tangos and a bit of Italian music.

At the beginning, tango was only danced in brothels and it was a long time before it entered the patios of the *conventillos* (see page 29), and even longer before it entered the houses of middle class families.

The first tangos were probably played in several places around the same time. The musicians played them in brothels or in academies, which were dancing halls, where people gathered to dance.

But although the tango had originated in brothels and in semi–criminal environments with musicians like the "Negro" Casimiro or the "Mulatto" Sinforoso, slowly it began to leave the suburbs.

"Romántico Bulincito"
E. Diseo · A. Gentile

"La Cumparsita"
P. Contursi
G. Matos Rodriguez

"Araca Paris"
C. Lenzi · R. Collazo

Many youths of well off families started going to these outlying neighbourhoods where they spent a grand time at the brothels. There they also had the chance of picking a quarrel, because for them quarrelling could also be fun.

Here they learnt to dance the tango.

Sheet Music Cover "Araca Paris"

On 24 March 2000, a new statue of Carlos Gardel by Mariano Pagés was inaugurated in Buenos Aires. It has been placed near the Abasto, the old Central Market. On the occasion an orchestra, conducted by Osvaldo Piro played tangos by Gardel and Le Pera.

Some of these youths danced the tango in Paris where it immediately generated a frenzy of enthusiasm in the ballrooms of the years 1913 and 1914.

This exotic and sensual dance which provided an excuse for close contact with a single partner, was immediately adopted by Parisians, who transformed it into an overpowering craze.

Everything was tango in Paris: the tango fashion introduced a new skirt with a long slit designed by the couturiers to facilitate the step; yellowish orange became the tango colour, tango tea parties were staged in hotels and other gathering places to teach the new dance.

Italy, Germany and England did not want to lag behind and they quickly adopted the fashion. Argentine teachers founded academies all over Europe and in 1914 they took the tango to the United States.

But in spite of the frenzy there were many detractors who criticised tango as a wild and sensual dance. The German Kaiser forbade his officials to dance tango while they were in uniform. In Paris a scandalised countess asked if it wouldn't be better to dance tango in bed.

After the success in Paris, the tango returned to Argentina, becoming socially accepted, and the *orquesta típica*, (typical orchestra, formed by a violin, a piano and a bandoneon), moved from the brothel to the cabaret in the centre of Buenos Aires.

Anonimous, 1925

In 1963 the Buenos Aires Lunfardo Academy was created, (lunfardo is the slang of Buenos Aires), presided over by José Gobello and in 1990 composers, poets, historians and collectors formed the National Academy of the Tango, chaired by Horacio Ferrer.

The famous duet Gardel-Razzano sang for the first time in the Armenonville, one of the most elegant restaurant-cabarets with a dance floor in the city.

The *Guardia Vieja*, (Old Guard) as the musicians between 1880 and 1920 were known, were no academic performers (Roberto Firpo, Agustín Bardi, Francisco Canaro, Eduardo Arolas); most of them belonged to the first Argentine generation of Italian immigrants and they usually played improvisations on their instruments.

Their merit has been to have helped the tango gain a firm foothold and to have spread its popularity all over Europe and America.

In 1920 the tango, which had been spirited and lively at the beginning, became intensely melancholic. The musicians, most of them of Italian origin who had had the benefit of a musical education, introduced their own nostalgia and loneliness into the tango.

When Julio de Caro created his Sextet (a piano, two violins, two bandoneons and a contrabass) in 1924 the *Guardia Nueva* (New Guard) was inaugurated.

Polyphony and counterpoint were introduced and there was practically no place left for improvisation. Beside De Caro, among the leaders of this movement were Osvaldo Fresedo, Juan Carlos Cobián and Pedro Maffia.

In the 30s the orchestras became larger and their interpreters gained popularity through the radio and gramophone records. It is the time of Juan de Dios Filiberto and Juan D'Arienzo. Their tangos were more cheerful and they played to packed ballrooms.

Anibal Troilo

Anibal Troilo, Pichuco, "the Greatest Bandoneon in Buenos Aires", had his first orchestra in 1937 and his merit was the selection of excellent musicians, singers (Alberto Marino, Edmundo Rivero, Roberto Goyeneche), and arrangers. Troilo was an important composer and orchestra conductor, but he will always be remembered as the all-time great bandoneon player.

The tango had become massively successful.

The decade of the 40s belonged to Anibal Troilo and Osvaldo Pugliese.

In 1950 the vanguard led by Astor Piazzolla, Atilio Stampone and Horacio Salgán started playing their new music. The big orchestras were replaced by more reduced groups and the musicians began to give tango concerts. It was the era of the excellent soloists.

In 1985 a very successful show was performed in Broadway: *Tango Argentino* by Claudio Segovia and Héctor Orezzoli. This production was staged worldwide and it started a new tango fashion, which became more refined and sophisticated. It was the second time that the tango became a craze in the United States. In the 20s, Rudolph Valentino had danced tango in his films dressed as a gaucho.

The tango is danced in the entire world today, from Japan to the United States, from northern Europe to Buenos Aires, and thanks to Astor Piazzolla, the tango has been introduced in the concert hall: the Kronos Quartet, Mstislav Rostropovich, Daniel Barenboim, Yo Yo Ma, Gidon Kremer usually include a tango in their repertoire.

In Buenos Aires there has been a rebirth of tango. The 11 December (Gardel's birthday) has been declared the National Day of Tango.

Edouard Malouze
"Le Tango"
1919

Carlos Gardel (1887–1935)

"Gardel is mine, but I might lend him to you for a little while."
Horacio Ferrer

Carlos Gardel was the son of Marie Berthe Gardes and he was born in Toulouse, France. The date of his birth is not known for certain, but it was given on his identity card as 11 December 1887. This same card says that he was born in Tacuarembó, a city in Uruguay. There is no clear account of his life before 1912.

In the year 1925 Gardel sings in one of the biggest farms in Argentina, Huetel, for the Prince of Wales and the Maharajah of Kapurthala who accompanies him on his ukulele.

He began to sing in a bar called O'Rondemann in the neighbourhood of *El Abasto*, the old Central Market of Buenos Aires.

In December 1913 an influential personality, Pancho Taurel, heard him singing at a restaurant and took him to the Armenonville, the elegant cabaret in the centre of Buenos Aires. He was an immediate success. It is said that when the owner of the place told Gardel that he would pay him $70 a night, Gardel answerd that for that money he would also wash up. The duet Gardel–Razzano quickly became very famous.

Gardel, with his typical tango hairstyle sang in theatres and in films; he recorded countless disks and travelled to France, Spain and the United States. To all intents and purposes he became a symbol of Argentina. Tango was no longer a dance, it was also a song.

He died tragically in a plane crash in Colombia at the peak of his career and so unexpectedly that he immediately became a myth.

His luminous and indestructible smile together with his musicality, his generous personality, the kindness of his expression and his success, made him an immortal character.

The Structure of Tango

The tango is made up of 2 parts of 16 bars each. Although at the beginning there were tangos with 3 parts (the third part was called trio), from 1925 on, they were no longer written in 3 parts. Sometimes, introductions, bridge passages and codas are added.

The bar of the tango had its origins in the two-four time of the habanera, but today the tango is written in four-four time.

The structure is A B A B.

There are three types of tangos: the *tango-milonga* (a rhythmic, quick time dance, usually without words), the *tango-romanza* (a melody without words) and the *tango-canción* or tango with words (a simple melody with words).

Carlos Gardel by Hermenegildo Sabat, Stamp, 1985

Carlos Gardel by Carlos Alonso, Stamp, 1985

Nicolás Rubió "Tonight, I'll get drunk", 1995

The Orchestra

"The tango orchestra is purer and better
tuned than that of jazz, and the tango is a true work of art."
Erich Kleiber, Conductor at the Teatro Colón (1926-1949)

*Julio de Caro and
his sextet, 1926*

*In 1924 Julio de
Caro's "Historical
Sextet" (two violins,
two bandoneons, a
piano and a contra-
bass), inaugurates
the Guardia Nueva.
Tango became a
generic piece, a musi-
cal composition with
written rules. In
1937 the orchestra is
made up of eight
musicians (three
bandoneons, three
violins, piano and
contrabass), and in
1957 the electric
guitar was added.
The orchestra was
no longer a group of
musicians playing
in unison: each
soloist now demon-
strated his individ-
ual talents.*

**Eduardo Ungar
"Dance on the
Street"**

There is a chronicle from the year 1913 which says that the tango was played by the Negro Casimiro on his violin and the Mulatto Sinforoso on his clarinet. This singular duet possibly played without knowing how to read music, they improvised and played by ear.

As time went by the duets became trios: a flute, a violin and a guitar played by Italian immigrants or their descendants. They played in theatres and academies or in brothels where the prostitutes danced tango with the clients. These travelling musicians used easily transportable instruments.

These first trios were formed either by a flute, a violin and a guitar or two violins and a flute and the quartets added the *bandoneon*, responsible for a sadder, more nostalgic and deeper tango.

The bandoneon replaced the flute and the trios were then formed of a bandoneon, a violin and a guitar which in turn was displaced by the piano, giving the tango a more painful colour.

A piano, a violin and a bandoneon formed the *orquesta típica*. To mark the rhythm, a battery was added but it was displaced by a contrabass later on.

The contrabass introduced the *canyengue* effect produced by tapping the strings of the instrument with the hand or the arch, to produce the rhythm.

In 1916 the first quintets appeared (piano, two violins, bandoneon and flute). These were the orchestras that played in cabarets. The musicians no longer came from the *arrabal* (the utmost limit of the city), they had studied music and dressed in dinner jackets.

The Bandoneon

"When I play the bandoneon I am alone, or with everybody, which is more or less the same thing."
Anibal Troilo
(1914-1975)

The best bandoneon performers were Eduardo Arolas, Pedro Maffia, Pedro Laurenz, Anibal Troilo and Astor Piazzolla.

Heinrich Band from Krefeld, Germany, created the bandoneon in 1846. This new instrument was an improved concertina, which had been created in the early nineteenth century to replace the organ in small churches or for marriages outdoors; they already had a hexagonal form, typical of the bandoneon.

The first bandoneon had 64 tones but there were some that had up to 200 tones in 5 lines of studs. These studs were for both hands. The sound of the bandoneon is more serious and more painful than the sound of the accordion. It is not easy to play the bandoneon because it is a double-action instrument, its sound changes depending on whether the bandoneon is opened or closed. Inside there are two acoustic boxes and a system of metal reeds that are made to vibrate when the air flows around them.

The most common bandoneons have 144 tones and the best are those signed by Alfred Arnold, (AA). Since the factories that produced them no longer exist, today bandoneons are rare and collectors and musicians are keen on them.

The bandoneon, called *"the bellows"* in tango slang, is the perfect instrument to communicate sadness, nostalgia, melancholy and when the notes are dragged, it gives the tango the necessary strain to convey the idea that the music slides.

Astor Piazzolla (1921-1992)

*"I am fed up with people who say
that my music is not tango."*
Astor Piazzolla

Astor Piazzolla, was born in Mar del Plata, on 11 March 1921 but he spent his first years in Greenwich Village, New York. His father gave him his first bandoneon when he was 9 years old. When he returned to Buenos Aires, Aníbal Troilo accepted him in his orchestra and there he stayed until his arrangements, his music and his tangos, no longert fitted Troilo's style.

He began to scandalise the traditionalists: "I will never have and will never seek success among the majority", he said more than once, "I write difficult music, it is not for those who seek entertainment. It is a music to make people think."

He inherited polyrhythmy from Stravinsky, Villalobos and Bartok. His rhythm was frantic and vigorous, his harmonies were audacious. He reinvented the tango, giving it a definitive modernity.

He said once, that those accustomed to traditional tango hated him. "I introduced irreverence, people thought that I was crazy. The tango critics said that my music was paranoiac. That's how they made me popular. The youth that had lost interest in tango, began listening to me."

In 1960 he founded the *Quinteto Nuevo Tango* (bandoneon, piano, violin, electric guitar and contrabass) which became his ideal ensemble.

The tango has entered the concert hall with Piazzolla, and famous interpreters include his music in their concerts.

"Astor Piazzolla"
José Biasutto, 1982

The Archetypes of the Tango

At the very beginning, tango was danced by men. The *compadre*, the *compadrito* and the *malevo* are the three most important male archetypes of tango and were the first to dance it.

The *compadre* was a kind of urban *gaucho* feared and envied but who had earned respect and a feeling of admiration by his authority and courage. He could be a cart driver, a butcher, a man who broke in horses or some politician's bodyguard.

"Caminito"
Carlos Gardel

He always honoured his word and did not hesitate to draw his knife when his honour was at sake. Very independent and proud, he was dressed in black with a scarf around his neck and a vicuña shawl on his shoulder.

The *compadrito* was the imitator of the compadre but without his virtues. Although he was always willing to draw his knife because of a disrespectful look, he was fearful of his personal security. He spent his life making a show of his conquests and boasting about his fake temerity.

He was also dressed in black with a silken scarf but the jacket and the trousers were not necessarily made of the same cloth. The jacket was short with high shoulder pads and he carried it unbuttoned to be able to take the knife out of the armhole of his waistcoat. His boots were high heeled and his grey hat had a black ribbon, and to crown so much elegance he had a cigarette butt or a toothpick in his mouth.

"Guitarra Mía"
Carlos Gardel

In this gallery, the *malevo* was at the end of the scale. He was a tricky coward, insolent and rude; the malevo felt a deep-seated resentment against society.

The Words of Tango

" ...We could say, that these [the words of tango] form an unconnected and vast comédie humaine *of the life of Buenos Aires."*
Jorge Luis Borges, 1930.

All the desires, pains, sufferings, dreams of the *porteño* (the inhabitant of the City of Buenos Aires) are expressed in the tango.

The themes are stated with raw realism in a 3-minute song, which tells a story, usually a sad one. In the tango, the porteño summarises his philosophy.

The first tangos danced in the suburbs were simple and, more often than not, pornographic songs. They reflected the life of the underclass, making special references to the physical characteristics of the characters and using a humour dependent on innuendo.

At the beginning of the twentieth century, many tangos were just sarcastic monologues of conceited *compadritos* who presented themselves provocatively, demanding to be respected for all their *good* qualities,

Eduardo Ungar
"The Sentadita"
(Detail)

*"There is nobody in the whole world
Who dances better than me."*

*"Nobody is like me
When it comes to winning the love of women."*

But then, after 1920, the tango becomes sad and melancholic. The man, abandoned by his partner, gets drunk to forget,

*"I want to be happy with this wine
And see if the wine makes me forget."*

He complains bitterly about his loneliness,

*"Nothing in the world can heal my pain,
I am all alone with your ingratitude."*

The origin of so much sadness is often his lover's infidelity. Love in a tango always finishes in betrayal,

"But the night came, the days passed,
The months passed and she never returned."

The *porteño* can also be sad because the woman he has loved has left her humble home and, dazzled by riches, gives way to a life full of luxury,

"You are no longer my Margarita,
Now they call you Margot!"

The male character of the tango has neither father nor children. All his affection is therefore centred on his mother. She is the embodiment of all human virtues. His mother works for him; she is the only person willing to forgive him, the only person in the world that will never let him down,

Eduardo Ungar
"The Circle"
(Detail)

"Only a mother forgives us in this life.
That is true, the rest is a lie!"

The *porteño* feels sorry for himself, the world is indifferent to his sorrow,

"My friends don't come
They don't even visit me,
Nobody wants to console me
In my affliction."

"And that friendly dog
That didn't eat, after you left me,
As he saw me all alone
Has left me too."

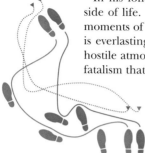

In his loneliness he is unable to see the positive side of life. Life is only a negative experience. The moments of happiness are ephemeral, only suffering is everlasting. Convinced that society has created a hostile atmosphere for him, he feels in his resigned fatalism that failure and poverty have trapped him,

"The salt of time has oxidized his face."

"You should never expect any help,
Nor a favour, nor a hand."

The limit between right and wrong is not precise. Tangos are sarcastic about this and reflect disenchantment,

"Today it is the same
To be honest or a traitor!
Ignorant, wise or a thief,
Generous, or a cheat."

Hope doesn't exist,

Miguel Ángel Biazzi
"In half-light"

"Today, I don't even believe in myself,
Everything is a lie, everything is false."

The café is the only place where he feels people will listen to him, it is there that he finds protection,

These are the principal tango steps. The dotted line shows the movements of the woman's feet. The basic figures are easy to master.

"I can't forget you in this complaint,
Café of Buenos Aires,
You are the only thing in this life,
That resembled my old mum."

There, one can chat about politics, football, about how difficult it is to make both ends meet.

But not everything is sadness and despair, friendship, a true virtue among Argentines, is mentioned in the tango,

"Remember that this friend,
Ready to risk his neck for you,
Will help you in what you need,
When the occasion arises."

Common places are constantly repeated, especially in the description of women,

"You were as pretty as the sun
They stopped to look at you."

"My girl was like a flower,
More beautiful than a golden day full of sun."

The tango has changed very much nowadays, the young poets have new themes: the mobile phone, stress, a heart attack, the freezer, the shopping mall, astronauts.

The character of the tango has learnt to be happy. Football, of course, is one of the sources of happiness,

"And that delirium of following my team
And the happiness exploding every goal!"

The tango is no longer "a hoarse lament of a bandoneon", the *porteño* has changed. He now knows that one has to conquer life day by day,

"I believe in my arms,
And in what they can give."

La Boca
In La Boca (the mouth), Buenos Aires becomes Naples. It is the colourful neighbourhood where the Riachuelo enters the Río de la Plata. It formed part of the arrabal in the nineteenth century.

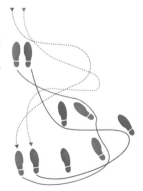

The Arrabal

"The Old Almacén"
by J. Cannella
Stamp

The *arrabal* is the suburb, the frontier between the city and the *pampa*.

In the suburbs of Buenos Aires, at the end of the nineteenth century, there was a large majority of men: the *gauchos* who had left the fields where they could not live freely anymore, the employees of the slaughterhouses, the cart drivers who came to the city with their products, the sailors who arrived at a port that exported more and more leather, meat and cereal, the immigrants who arrived hoping that Argentina would be the solution to all their problems.

"The Barrel Organ
Player"
by A. Severi
Stamp, 1982

Immigrants Hotel,
1905

The Conventillos

The *conventillos* were long houses with small rooms that opened onto a common patio. In their origin, these constructions had been houses of well off families that had moved to the northern part of Buenos Aires after the terrible epidemic of yellow fever in 1871.

The mixture of languages and customs, the lack of hygiene and privacy, made the conventillo a sordid place.

It was in that central patio where the tango was often danced and sung to the sounds of a barrel organ or to improvised musicians with a guitar, a violin or a flute.

Immigrants
At the end of the nineteenth century Buenos Aires received many immigrants. Three out of every four persons living in Buenos Aires in 1914 were European-born. These immigrants, who came mainly from Italy and Spain, were, in their majority, lone men. They all lived stacked in conventillos in the southern part of the city, in the arrabal, the frontier between Buenos Aires and the Pampa.

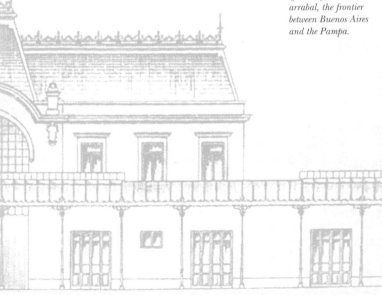

Dancing Tango

"The tango is a sad thought danced"
Enrique Santos Discépolo (1901-1951)

The most famous woman singers were Sofía Bozán, Mercedes Simone, Nelly Omar, Azucena Maizani, Libertad Lamarque, Tania, Tita Merello, María Graña, Amelita Baltar, Eladia Blázquez and Susana Rinaldi.

The success of the tango is due to the way in which it is danced.

When dancing tango, the man holds the woman tightly because "we either hug each other tightly or we step on each other".

Although it is said that the tango is a dance full of lust and aggressiveness and that it expresses the dancer's sexual instincts, it is not so much lust but concentration and mutual understanding that are needed in order to be able to dance it.

The tango demands a minimum of effort, it is the art of knowing how to walk, how to drag the feet. The woman has to be very attentive to be able to follow the man and his changing will. With a simple pressure of his hand on her waist, he will lead his partner.

In the tango there is no choreography, everything is decided on the spur of the moment: if the step is indolent and lethargic, voluptuous and sensual, if suddenly the displacement is suspended and the couple remains still, or the man stops and the woman rotates or prances, if they walk face to face or side-ways or backwards.

In the *corte* (a cut), prelude to a *quebrada*, the march is cut, there is a sudden pause, the *quebrada* is a contortion, as if the body would break.

The couple that dances tango does not chat, she has to be very attentive to the marks he uses to indicate her displacements, she has to feel his intentions.

Eduardo Ungar
"Two Sisters",
(detail)
"Tango Club"

Index

Omar and Cristina in their Tango Show

*"This is the tango, song of Buenos Aires,
born in the suburb, to reign in the whole world"*
Manuel Romero